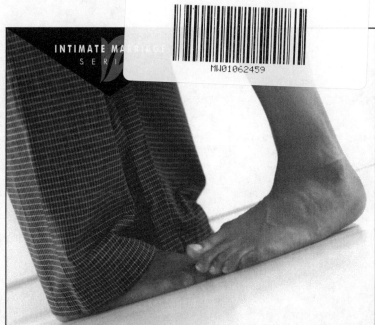

INTIMATE MARRIAGE
SERIES

MALE AND FEMALE

Dan B. Allender
and Tremper Longman III

6 STUDIES FOR INDIVIDUALS, COUPLES OR GROUPS

InterVarsity Press
Downers Grove, Illinois

InterVarsity Press
P.O. Box 1400, Downers Grove, IL 60515-1426
World Wide Web: www.ivpress.com
E-mail: mail@ivpress.com

InterVarsity Press® is the book-publishing division of InterVarsity Christian Fellowship/USA®, a student movement active on campus at hundreds of universities, colleges and schools of nursing in the United States of America, and a member movement of the International Fellowship of Evangelical Students. For information about local and regional activities, write Public Relations Dept., InterVarsity Christian Fellowship/USA, 6400 Schroeder Rd., P.O. Box 7895, Madison, WI 53707-7895, or visit the IVCF website at <www.intervarsity.org>.

Unless otherwise indicated, all Scripture quotations are taken from the Holy Bible, *New Living Translation, copyright ©1996, 2004. Used by permission of Tyndale House Publishers, Inc., Wheaton, Illinois 60189. All rights reserved.*

Design: Cindy Kiple

Images: Ryan McVay/Getty Images

ISBN 0-8308-2134-1

Printed in the United States of America ∞

P	18	17	16	15	14	13	12	11	10	9	8	7	6	5	4	3	2	1
Y	18	17	16	15	14	13	12	11	10	09	08	07	06	05				

CONTENTS

WELCOME TO
INTIMATE MARRIAGE
BIBLE STUDIES

MALE AND FEMALE

You are about to embark on an important and rather controversial subject: gender. What is the difference, besides the obvious, between a man and a woman? Or do you think there are differences at all? If such differences exist, then it would be important for husbands to know something about their wives as females and for wives to know something about their husbands as males.

Christians are often passionately divided on the topic of gender, so it is good to investigate the key passages in the discussion. What is a male and what is a female, and what makes a good husband and what makes a good wife? The following studies will provide an opportunity for you to reach answers on these important questions.

TAKING MARRIAGE SERIOUSLY

Most of us want to have a good marriage. Those who don't have a good relationship yearn for a better one, and those who have a good one want even more intimacy.

We want to know our spouse and be known by them. We want to be loved and to love. In short, we want the type of marriage desired by God from the beginning when he created the institution of marriage and defined it as involving leaving parents, weaving a life of intimacy together and cleaving in sexual bliss.

These studies delve into the wisdom of the Bible in order to learn what it takes to have not just a "good" marriage but one that enjoys the relational richness that God intended for a husband and a wife. This divinely instituted type of marriage is one that will

- Bring a husband and wife closer together
- Understand that marriage is one's primary loyalty to other human beings
- Be characterized by a growing love and knowledge of one another
- Be an arena of spiritual growth
- Allow for the healthy exposure of sin through the offer of forgiveness
- Be a crucible for showing grace
- Reflect God's love for his people
- Enjoy God's gift of sexual intimacy
- Share life's joys and troubles
- Have a part in transforming us from sinners to saints
- Bring out each other's glory as divine image bearers

And so much more! The Bible provides a wealth of insight, and these studies hope to tap its riches and bring them to bear on our marriage relationships.

USING THE STUDIES

These studies can be used in a variety of contexts—individual devotional life, by a couple together or by a small group—or in a combination of these settings. Each study includes the following components.

Open. Several quotes at the beginning give a sense of what married people say about the topic at hand. These are followed by a question that can be used for discussion. If you are using the DVD, you may want to skip this and go straight to the opening clip.

DVD Reflection. For each session we have an opening thought from Dan Allender, at times accompanied by an excerpt from our interviews with married couples, to get you thinking about the topic at hand. This material will provide fresh and engaging openers for a small group as well as interesting discussion points for couples studying together. You will find a question here to discuss after you watch the DVD clip.

Study. One or more key Bible texts are included in the guide for convenience. We have chosen the New Living Translation, but you may use any version of Scripture you like. The questions in this section will take you through the key aspects of the passage and help you apply them to your marriage. Sprinkled throughout the study, you will also find commentary to enrich your experience.

For the Couple. Here's an opportunity to make an application and commitment, which is specific to your marriage.

Bonus. These are further ideas for study on your own. Or if you are studying with a group, take time to do the bonus item with your spouse during the week.

We hope that these studies enrich your marriage. We encourage you to be brutally honest with yourself and tactfully honest with your spouse. If you are willing to be honest with yourself and with the Scripture, then God will do great things for your marriage. That is our prayer.

GENDER DIFFERENCES

"I just don't understand her. Why does she cry when I say that?"

"He never talks to me. He stays in his shell."

"She always wants to go out and be with other people. I enjoy staying at home with her and the kids."

"Men are from Mars, women are from Venus."

▶ OPEN

Women, how do you think men are different from women? Men, what general differences do you see between women and men? Share your perceptions with each other.

▶ DVD REFLECTION

What is helpful or valuable about the differences between men and women that you see?

▶ STUDY

We know that men and women are different—even beyond

anatomy. But precisely how are they different, and how do we recognize the differences in a marriage? To explore these questions, we turn to perhaps an unlikely text, God's judgments on Adam and Eve given in consequence of their sin of eating the fruit of the tree of the knowledge of good and evil. The nature of these curses reveals some of the differences between male and female.

Read Genesis 3:16-19.

[16]Then he said to the woman,
>   "I will sharpen the pain of your pregnancy
>   and in pain you will give birth.
>   And you will desire to control your husband,
>   but he will rule over you."

[17]And to the man he said,
>   "Since you listened to your wife and ate from the tree
>   whose fruit I commanded you not to eat,
>   the ground is cursed because of you.
>   All your life you will struggle to scratch a living from it.
[18]It will grow thorns and thistles for you,
>   though you will eat of its grains.
[19]By the sweat of your brow
>   will you have food to eat
>   until you return to the ground
>   from which you were made.
>   For you were made from dust,
>   and to dust you will return.

1. Look at the curse directed toward Eve. In what areas of her life does God's punishment affect her?

2. How have you seen these effects of the Fall reflected in your own experience?

3. Look at the curse directed toward Adam. In what areas of his life does it affect him?

4. Again, how have you seen these effects of the Fall reflected in your experience?

5. If women are generally more focused on relationship and men

on work, what characteristics is each gender most likely to display?

6. Does this mean that men aren't concerned with relationship nor women with work? Explain.

Does it mean that the Bible lays down distinct roles for men and women? Explain.

7. Is it better or worse to marry someone like yourself? Explain your response.

8. How can differences either enhance or hurt a marriage?

▶ FOR THE COUPLE

In what way is your spouse similar to and dissimilar from you? Talk about the differences that bring joy. Then talk about those that bring struggle. How do you honor and grow the differences you enjoy? Do you sometimes withdraw or use contempt against the differences that trouble you? What would happen if you were to bless the differences that most unnerve you?

▶ BONUS

Chapter two of Mary Stewart Van Leeuwen's *Gender and Grace: Love, Work and Parenting in a Changing World* (InterVarsity Press) describes the effects of the Fall and how sin tends to drive men and women apart. Read this chapter together and discuss its insights.

WHO'S IN CHARGE?

"The man is the head of the household. The buck stops with the head."

"Women are too emotional to be leaders; it takes clearheaded men to make important decisions that affect the family."

"Jesus was a man, not a woman. And so were all the disciples."

▶ OPEN

Few, if any, would say the Bible teaches that men are inherently superior to women. But many think that God has created a social order that requires men to lead and women to follow in the household. What do you think?

▶ DVD REFLECTION

Who's in charge at your house?

▶ STUDY

This passage fits into an argument that Paul makes against those

Christians who regard keeping the law as foundational to a relationship with God. It is faith in Jesus—not the law—which establishes a relationship with the divine. We are no longer slaves to the law but children of God!

Read Galatians 3:26—4:7.

[26]For you are all children of God though faith in Christ Jesus. [27]And all who have been united with Christ in baptism have put on the character of Christ, like putting on new clothes. [28]There is no longer Jew or Gentile, slave or free, male and female. For you are all one in Christ Jesus. [29]And now that you belong to Christ, you are the true children of Abraham. You are his heirs, and God's promise to Abraham belongs to you.

4 Think of it this way. If a father dies and leaves an inheritance for his young children, those children are not much better off than slaves until they grow up, even though they actually own everything their father had. [2]They have to obey their guardians until they reach whatever age their father set. [3]And that's the way it was with us before Christ came. We were like children; we were slaves to the basic spiritual principles of this world.

[4]But when the right time came, God sent his Son, born of a woman, subject to the law. [5]God sent him to buy freedom for us who were slaves to the law, so that he could adopt us as his very own children. [6]And because we are his children, God has sent the Spirit of his Son into our hearts, prompting us to call out, "Abba, Father." [7]Now you are no longer a slave but God's own child. And since you are his child, God has made you his heir.

1. According to Paul, what eradicates the established hierarchies of the day?

2. Why does Paul list the "male-female" dichotomy with "Jew-Gentile" and "slave-free"?

3. What social hierarchies do you see operating in our culture?

4. Does the equality of men and women mean that the genders are exactly alike? Explain.

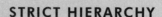

STRICT HIERARCHY

In the first-century world of Paul's time, certain strict hierarchies were observed. These hierarchies were ethnic (Jew-Gentile), social (free-slave) and gendered (male-female). Indeed, an early Jewish writing called the Tosefta preserves a saying that may come from Paul's time: "Blessed be God that he did not make me a Gentile; blessed be God that he did not make me a slave; blessed be God that he did not make me a woman" (Tosefta Berakot 7:18). Paul's message is that in Christ these hierarchies are no longer to divide or be the basis of a difference in honor or power.

5. What happens in a marriage when the husband feels superior or in charge of his spouse?

6. Do women sometimes take the upper hand and assert dominance over men in a marriage? Explain your response.

7. Is equality between a husband and wife true *only* in Christ? That is, does gender equality have meaning only on a spiritual level, or does it have practical applications? Explain.

8. What does equality between a husband and wife look like?

▶ **FOR THE COUPLE**

Discuss specific situations in which your spouse treated you as an equal. How can your marriage grow in this area? What does it mean to treat your spouse as an equal at times

- when you think your spouse is wrong?
- when you think your spouse is weak?
- when you agree one spouse knows more than the other?

▶ **BONUS**

Read the passages that tell of a married couple who ministered alongside the apostle Paul: Priscilla and Aquila (Acts 18:1-3, 18-28; Romans 16:3-5; 1 Corinthians 16:19; 2 Timothy 4:19). Where do you see evidence of equality in their marriage and ministry?

3

THE TEN-LETTER
DIRTY WORD:
S-U-B-M-I-S-S-I-O-N

"Do you promise to submit and obey . . . till death do you part?"

"How can I trust another person enough to submit to them? I have to stay in charge of my life."

"He treats me as a common slave and justifies it by telling me the Bible says a wife must submit to her husband. I want to obey the Bible, but this is so demeaning."

"I know the Bible says that a wife must submit to her husband, but doesn't it also say somewhere that we are all to submit to each other? How does that work out?"

▶ OPEN

Nothing unsettles modern women and men more than the biblical call to submit. Such protest may be motivated by the North American drive to be in control of one's own life. *No one can tell me what to do. I am my own boss.* What do you think?

▶ DVD REFLECTION

What do you think of how Dan Allender defines submission?

▶ STUDY

We need to consider carefully whether we understand the biblical teaching correctly. What does the Bible really say about submission in the context of marriage?

Read Ephesians 5:21-33.

[21]And further, submit to one another out of reverence for Christ.

[22]For wives, this means submit to your husbands as to the Lord. [23]For a husband is the head of his wife as Christ is the head of the church. He is the Savior of his body, the church. [24]As the church submits to Christ, so you wives should submit to your husbands in everything.

[25]For husbands, this means love your wives just as Christ loved the church. He gave up his life for her [26]to make her holy and clean, washed by the cleansing of God's word. [27]He did this to present her to himself as a glorious church without a spot or wrinkle or any other blemish. Instead, she will be holy and without fault. [28]In the same way, husbands ought to love their wives as they love their own bodies. For a man who loves his wife actually shows love for himself. [29]No one hates his own body but feeds and cares for it, just as Christ cares for the church. [30]And we are members of his body.

[31]As the Scriptures say, "A man leaves his father and mother and is joined to his wife, and the two are united into one." [32]This is a great mystery, but it is an illustration of the way Christ and the church are one. [33]So again I say, each man must love his wife as he loves himself, and the wife must respect her husband.

Read Philippians 2:3-4.

³Don't be selfish; don't try to impress others. Be humble, thinking of others as better than yourselves. ⁴Don't look out only for your own affairs, but take an interest in others, too.

▼

NEWFOUND FREEDOM

Everything we know about the Jewish and Hellenistic cultures of the days of the early church suggests that women had few rights. In the light of its original context, then, the gospel was nothing short of liberating for women. It is important to remember this context as we study Ephesians 5 and other New Testament texts that call on women to submit to their husbands.

1. Ephesians 5:21 exhorts all Christians to submit to each other, and verse 22 then specifically calls on wives to submit to their husbands. Is there a contradiction here? Explain.

2. How does Paul say husbands are supposed to treat their wives?

3. Has any husband in your family background—perhaps your father, grandfather, uncle—done an especially good job at treating his wife as Paul instructs? Recount one incident as an example.

4. Based on Paul's teaching for husbands, what does it mean for the husband to be the head of the wife?

Is Paul saying that women are to be subordinate to their husbands? Explain.

5. What happens to a marriage in which either spouse lords it over the other?

6. What happens to a marriage in which either spouse abdicates all responsibility to love and guide the other?

7. What does it mean to submit in a relationship? (Does submission mean always doing what the other person says or never making demands of the other?)

8. What would a marriage inspired by Philippians 2:3-4 look like?

▶ **FOR THE COUPLE**

Study 1 Peter 3:1-6 together. What does Sarah's relationship with Abraham tell us about submission?

▶ **BONUS**

Philippians 2:3-4 is followed by an account of Jesus as the su-
preme exemplar of the attitude Christians should have toward
each other (Philippians 2:5-11). Study this powerful text and ask
what kinds of changes would take place in a marriage where husband and wife thought and acted toward each other in this way.

THE GODLY WIFE

"I work and I have a family. Sometimes I feel so torn between those two worlds I just don't know what to do."

"He says I should lose twenty pounds. He says it is my responsibility to meet his sexual needs. I raise our three kids and work part time. I would love to lose twenty pounds, but it hurts me to think that that is so important to him."

"A woman's place is in the home."

▶ OPEN

What's a woman to do? There has never been a time that put such huge burdens on females. A stay-at-home mom feels disrespected by her working friends. A woman who works may feel guilty about the time away from her family. All this, and her husband expects gourmet meals and exciting sex. Are such demands biblical? Why or why not?

▶ DVD REFLECTION

What do you find surprising or challenging or refreshing about how Dan Allender describes the godly wife?

▶ STUDY

What does the Bible say is the most important thing that a woman can do and be? The following passage is the Hebrew equivalent of an A to Z on the capable and virtuous woman. The passage is an acrostic: each verse begins with a different letter of the Hebrew alphabet, and the twenty-two letters are used in sequence. The idea is that here is a complete, even exhaustive description of the virtuous woman.

Read Proverbs 31:10-31.

[10]Who can find a virtuous and capable wife?
  She is more precious than rubies.
[11]Her husband can trust her,
  and she will greatly enrich his life.
[12]She brings him good, not harm,
  all the days of her life.

[13]She finds wool and flax
  and busily spins it.
[14]She is like a merchant's ship;
  bringing her food from afar.
[15]She gets up before dawn to prepare breakfast for her household
  and plan the day's work for her servant girls.

[16]She goes out to inspect a field and buys it;
  with her earnings she plants a vineyard.
[17]She is energetic and strong,
  a hard worker.
[18]She makes sure her dealings are profitable;
  her lamp burns late into the night.

[19]Her hands are busy spinning thread,
  her fingers twisting fiber.
[20]She extends a helping hand to the poor
  and opens her arms to the needy.
[21]She has no fear of winter for her household
  for everyone has warm clothes.

[22]She makes her own bedspreads.
  She dresses in fine linen and purple gowns.
[23]Her husband is well known at the city gates,
  where he sits with the other civic leaders.
[24]She makes belted linen garments
  and sashes to sell to the merchants.

[25]She is clothed with strength and dignity,
  and she laughs without fear of the future.
[26]When she speaks, her words are wise,
  and she gives instructions with kindness.
[27]She carefully watches everything in her household
  and suffers nothing from laziness.

[28]Her children stand and bless her.
  Her husband praises her:
[29]"There are many virtuous and capable women in the world,
  but you surpass them all!"

[30]Charm is deceptive, and beauty does not last;
  but a woman who fears the LORD will be greatly praised.
[31]Reward her for all she has done.
  Let her deeds publicly declare her praise.

1. After reading the whole passage, what are your initial impressions of the description of the "virtuous and capable wife"? (If you are in a group made up of both men and women, let the men answer this question first and let the women answer second.)

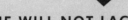

HE WILL NOT LACK PLUNDER

English translations render the second half of Proverbs 31:11 in different ways, and many obscure its military nuance. But when one looks at the Hebrew here, it is hard to explain away the statement that the husband will benefit from his wife's efforts because she provides him with plunder! The Hebrew word points to profits gained from waging war.

This is not the only place where the poem uses military language. Indeed, the Hebrew phrase for "capable and virtuous wife" contains a word used elsewhere in the Bible to describe the valor of soldiers.

Why would the Scriptures employ language that suggests warfare in its description of the woman? The Scriptures picture life as war. Since the Fall, the world is a place of chaos, and to make progress on behalf of order and goodness, one must fight the good fight. So marriage may be understood as an intimate alliance between a man and a woman who together engage a difficult and often hostile world. They do so in the presence and with the power of God (Ephesians 6:10-20).

2. Are you surprised by any unexpected characteristic of the woman in this description? Explain.

Do you notice a lack of some characteristic that you would have expected to see? Explain.

3. *For women only:* do you find this description of the "virtuous and capable wife" liberating or oppressive. Why?

4. Do you think this description is a requirement for all women who are godly, or do you think it is more like a catalog of options for women? Explain.

5. According to this poem, what is the single most important characteristic of the godly woman? Explain.

▼

WOMAN WISDOM AND THE
CAPABLE AND VIRTUOUS WOMAN

Proverbs 31 ends the book of Proverbs with a description of the capable and virtuous woman. By this time, the book has described various kinds of women at great length; after all, the original audience for the teaching of the book was the writer's son, a young man of marriageable age. The teaching of chapter 31 provides a culmination of the description of virtuous women who are the opposite of promiscuous women (see Proverbs 5).

In addition to frequent descriptions of human women throughout the book, there is much talk about and from a woman whose name is Wisdom (Proverbs 1:20-33; 8:1—9:6). She is a poetic personification of God's wisdom. It is interesting that the woman described in chapter 31 shares many of the characteristics of Woman Wisdom. In other words, the godly woman reflects the nature of God himself.

6. Does this mean that beauty and charm should be despised? Why or why not?

7. *For men only:* how would you describe the ideal woman?

Specifically, what is most important to you in a woman?

8. So "who *can* find a capable and virtuous wife" (see verse 10)?

▶ **FOR THE COUPLE**

Wife, talk with your husband about what keeps you from reaching your potential as a woman and wife. Husband, talk about what keeps you from helping her reach her potential in these areas:

- tenderness
- strength
- intellectual pursuits
- physical health
- play
- friendship
- career
- risk

▶ **BONUS**

Read and discuss Luke 11:27-28.

What is the woman saying about women's identity?

How does Jesus seek to refocus her thinking?

If you have children—or if you aspire to have children—in what ways have you been tempted to think like this woman?

How could your church's ministry to women help them gain a healthy sense of identity centered on the fear of the Lord?

THE GODLY HUSBAND

"He's good looking, and he makes a lot of money. Quite a catch."

"He's well respected at the company, and he's a member of the country club."

"Sometimes I don't know what is important. I have all the things the world says are important, but I still feel puny and insignificant."

▶ OPEN

What does it mean to be a good husband? In this day and age the signals are often mixed. Is it the husband who makes the decisions, earns good money and manages the household? What qualities are important—leadership, competence, intelligence? What are a man's proper goals—to make a lot of money, to have a respectable family, prestige, power?

▶ DVD REFLECTION

How does a godly man treat his family?

▶STUDY

Interestingly, Psalm 112 is stylistically parallel to Proverbs 31, perhaps intentionally so. It offers the A to Z of the godly husband.
The NLT and other translations have obscured one important as-
pect of Psalm 112 when it translates the object of its description in
a generic way. The poem concerns the godly man in particular,
not godly people. The questions in this study, then, require that
we read Psalm 112 as specifically directed toward men.

Read Psalm 112.

[1] Praise the LORD!
How joyful are those who fear the LORD
   and delight in obeying his commands.
[2] Their children will be successful everywhere;
   an entire generation of godly people will be blessed.
[3] They themselves will be wealthy,
   and their good deeds will last forever.
[4] Light shines in the darkness for the godly.
   They are generous, compassionate, and righteous.
[5] Good comes to those who lend money generously
   and conduct their business fairly.
[6] Such people will not be overcome by evil.
   Those who are righteous will be long remembered.
[7] They do not fear bad news;
   they confidently trust the LORD to care for them.
[8] They are confident and fearless
   and can face their foes triumphantly.

⁹ They share freely and give generously to those in need.

Their good deeds will be remembered forever.

They will have influence and honor.

¹⁰ The wicked will see this and be infuriated.

They will grind their teeth in anger;

they will slink away, their hopes thwarted.

1. According to Psalm 112, what is the most important trait of the godly man?

2. Reflect on the previous study of Proverbs 31. What traits are shared by the godly man and the godly woman?

3. *For men only:* does Psalm 112 match your vision of what it means to be a godly man? Explain.

Where does it make you feel burdened?

In what ways does it invite you to be free?

How do you handle those two different feelings?

4. What effect does a man's godliness have on his wife?

5. What characteristics are missing from this description of the godly man?

Can we draw significance from their absence? Explain.

6. Read Psalm 111 in the light of 112. There are many echoes between the two. Psalm 111 is another acrostic poem (see "A to Z, Again" sidebar), and many of 111's descriptions of God are applied to the godly man in 112. What are we to make of this?

7. If the godly man reflects the traits of God, then what must one do to be godly?

▶ **FOR THE COUPLE**

Husband, talk with your wife about what keeps you from reaching your potential as a man and husband. Wife, talk about what keeps you from helping him reach his potential in these areas:

- tenderness
- strength
- intellectual pursuits
- physical health
- play
- friendship
- career
- risk

▶ BONUS

Wild at Heart by John Elderidge is a tremendously popular book in which the author describes what he thinks the Bible means about being a man. Read this controversial book with an open and a critical mind. Discuss what you think reflects a biblical view of the man and what you think may be overblown or wrong.

REFLECTING THE GLORY OF GOD TOGETHER

"Some religions teach that men reflect the nature of God more than women do. They even say that godly women are turned into men when they get to heaven. What do Christians believe?"

"The Bible is so male oriented. It even pictures God as masculine, doesn't it?"

▶ OPEN

Many people think that the Bible presents a very male-oriented picture of who God is. Are they right? Is God male, female or no gender at all? What do the biblical depictions of God's gender teach us about marriage?

▶ DVD REFLECTION

What are you learning about God from each other?

▶ STUDY

God is beyond our highest thoughts. The psalmist cries out,

"Lord, who can compare with you?" (Psalm 35:10). The Bible describes the nature of God adequately but not exhaustively, and it does so by comparison, that is with metaphor and simile. While God can be described by comparison to an inanimate object or quality (such as light or a rock) or even an animal (bear or lion), the biblical authors most often have recourse to human beings. God is a king, a warrior, a mother, a father, a woman teacher, a shepherd—the list goes on and on. Human beings are appropriate means of teaching about the nature of God, because we are made in his image. We reflect his glory.

Read Joshua 5:13-15.

[13]When Joshua was near the town of Jericho, he looked up and saw a man standing in front of him with sword in hand. Joshua went up to him and demanded, "Are you friend or foe?"

[14]"Neither one," he replied. "I am commander of the Lord's army."

At this Joshua fell with his face to the ground in reverence. "I am at your command," Joshua said. "What do you want your servant to do?"

[15]The commander of the Lord's army replied, "Take off your sandals, for the place where you are standing is holy." And Joshua did as he was told.

Read Psalm 131.

[1]Lord, my heart is not proud;
  my eyes are not haughty.

I don't concern myself with matters too great
or awesome for me to grasp.
²Instead I have calmed and quieted myself,
like a weaned child who no longer cries for its mother's milk.
Yes, like a weaned child is my soul within me.
³O Israel, put your hope in the LORD—
now and always.

1. Who is the man with the sword in his hand in the Joshua 5 passage?

How do you know?

2. Does this image fit with your own mental images of God? Why or why not?

3. What do we learn about the nature of God from the Joshua story?

4. Does this portrait tell us anything about the gender of God? Explain.

Does it tell us anything about the nature of men? Explain.

GENDER: A PART OF CREATION, NOT OF THE CREATOR

Genesis 1:26-27 teaches us that God created all human beings, male and female:

> Then God said, "Let us make people in our image, to be like ourselves. They will be masters over all life—the fish of the sea, the birds in the sky, and all the livestock, wild animals, and small animals.
>
> So God created people in his own image;
> God patterned them after himself,
> male and female he created them.

Here we see that gender is a part of the creation, not the Creator. Both male and female are created in God's image. They each together and uniquely reflect the true nature of God.

5. What is the image presented in Psalm 131:2?

6. Why does the psalm specify that the child is weaned?

7. Does this portrait tell us anything about the gender of God? Explain.

Does it tell us anything about the nature of women? Explain.

8. The Bible represents God by metaphors of both genders. What meaning does that have for your own marriage?

▶ FOR THE COUPLE

What qualities of God do you see reflected in your spouse? Spend some time telling each other about those qualities and remembering times when they were particularly evident.

▶ BONUS

Read Revelation 19:6-8.

When God's relationship to his people is likened to a marriage, why do you think God is always pictured as the male?

Does this mean that God is closer to males than to females? Explain.

What does this picture teach us about marriage?

LEADER'S NOTES

My grace is sufficient for you.

2 CORINTHIANS 12:9 NIV

Leading a Bible discussion can be an enjoyable and rewarding experience. But it can also be *scary*—especially if you've never done it before. If this is your feeling, you're in good company. When God asked Moses to lead the Israelites out of Egypt, he replied, "O Lord, please send someone else to do it" (Ex 4:13 NIV). It was the same with Solomon, Jeremiah and Timothy, but God helped these people in spite of their weaknesses, and he will help you as well.

You don't need to be an expert on the Bible or a trained teacher to lead a Bible discussion. The idea behind these inductive studies is that the leader guides group members to discover for themselves what the Bible has to say. This method of learning will allow group members to remember much more of what is said than a lecture would.

These studies are designed to be led easily. As a matter of fact, the flow of questions through the passage from observation to interpretation to application is so natural that you may feel that the studies lead themselves. This study guide is also flexible. You can use it with a variety of groups—student, professional, neighborhood or church groups. Each study takes forty-five to sixty minutes in a group setting.

There are some important facts to know about group dynamics and encouraging discussion. The suggestions listed below should enable you to effectively and enjoyably fulfill your role as leader.

PREPARING FOR THE STUDY

1. Ask God to help you understand and apply the passage in your own life. Unless this happens, you will not be prepared to lead others. Pray too for the various members of the group. Ask God to open your hearts to the message of his Word and motivate you to action.

2. Read the introduction to the entire guide to get an overview of the entire book and the issues which will be explored.

3. As you begin each study, read and reread the assigned Bible passage to familiarize yourself with it.

4. This study guide is based on the New Living Translation of the Bible. It will help you and the group if you use this translation as the basis for your study and discussion.

5. Carefully work through each question in the study. Spend time in meditation and reflection as you consider how to respond.

6. Write your thoughts and responses in the space provided in the study guide. This will help you to express your understanding of the passage clearly.

7. It might help to have a Bible dictionary handy. Use it to look up any unfamiliar words, names or places. (For additional help on how to study a passage, see chapter five of *How to Lead a LifeGuide Bible Study*, InterVarsity Press.)

8. Consider how you can apply the Scripture to your life. Remember that the group will follow your lead in responding to the studies. They will not go any deeper than you do.

9. Once you have finished your own study of the passage, familiarize yourself with the leader's notes for the study you are leading. These are designed to help you in several ways. First, they tell you the purpose the study guide author had in mind when writing the study. Take time to think through how the study questions work together to accomplish that purpose. Second, the notes provide you with additional background information or suggestions on group dynamics for various questions. This information can be useful when people have difficulty understanding or answering a question. Third, the leader's notes can alert you to potential problems you may encounter during the study.

10. If you wish to remind yourself of anything mentioned in the leader's notes, make a note to yourself below that question in the study.

LEADING THE STUDY

1. Begin the study on time. Open with prayer, asking God to help the group to understand and apply the passage.

2. Be sure that everyone in your group has a study guide. Encourage the group to prepare beforehand for each discussion by reading the introduction to the guide and by working through the questions in the study.

3. At the beginning of your first time together, explain that these
    studies are meant to be discussions, not lectures. Encourage
    the members of the group to participate. However, do not put
    pressure on those who may be hesitant to speak during the
    first few sessions. You may want to suggest the following
    guidelines to your group.

    • Stick to the topic being discussed.

    • Your responses should be based on the verses that are the fo-
      cus of the discussion and not on outside authorities such as
      commentaries or speakers.

    • Anything said in the group is considered confidential and
      will not be discussed outside the group unless specific per-
      mission is given to do so.

    • Listen attentively to each other and provide time for each
      person present to talk.

    • Pray for each other.

4. Play the DVD clip from the *Intimate Marriage DVD* and use the
    DVD reflection question to kick off group discussion. You can
    move directly from there to the beginning of the study section.
    Or, if you wish, you can also have a group member read the in-
    troduction aloud and then you can discuss the question in the
    "Open" section. If you do not have the DVD, then be sure to
    kick off the discussion with the question in the "Open" section.

    The "Open" question and the DVD clip are meant to be used
    before the passage is read. They introduce the theme of the
    study and encourage members to begin to open up. Encourage

as many members as possible to participate, and be ready to get the discussion going with your own response.

This section is designed to reveal where your thoughts or feelings need to be transformed by Scripture. That is why it is especially important not to read the passage before the discussion question is asked. The passage will tend to color the honest reactions people would otherwise give because they are, of course, supposed to think the way the Bible does.

5. Have a group member (or members if the passage is long) read aloud the passage to be studied. Then give people several minutes to read the passage again silently so that they can take it all in.

6. Question 1 will generally be an overview question designed to briefly survey the passage. Encourage the group to look at the whole passage, but try to avoid getting sidetracked by questions or issues that will be addressed later in the study.

7. As you ask the questions, keep in mind that they are designed to be used just as they are written. You may simply read them aloud. Or you may prefer to express them in your own words.

There may be times when it is appropriate to deviate from the study guide. For example, a question may have already been answered. If so, move on to the next question. Or someone may raise an important question not covered in the guide. Take time to discuss it, but try to keep the group from going off on tangents.

8. The sidebars contain further background information on the texts in the study. If they are relevant to the course of your dis-

cussion, you may want to read them aloud. However, to keep the discussion moving, you may want to omit them and allow group members to read them on their own.

9. Avoid answering your own questions. If necessary, repeat or rephrase them until they are clearly understood. Or point out something you read in the leader's notes to clarify the context or meaning. An eager group quickly becomes passive and silent if they think the leader will do most of the talking.

10. Don't be afraid of silence. People may need time to think about the question before formulating their answers.

11. Don't be content with just one answer. Ask, "What do the rest of you think?" or "Anything else?" until several people have given answers to the question.

12. Acknowledge all contributions. Try to be affirming whenever possible. Never reject an answer. If it is clearly off-base, ask, "Which verse led you to that conclusion?" or again, "What do the rest of you think?"

13. Don't expect every answer to be addressed to you, even though this will probably happen at first. As group members become more at ease, they will begin to truly interact with each other. This is one sign of healthy discussion.

14. Don't be afraid of controversy. It can be very stimulating. If you don't resolve an issue completely, don't be frustrated. Move on and keep it in mind for later. A subsequent study may solve the problem.

15. Periodically summarize what the group has said about the

passage. This helps to draw together the various ideas mentioned and gives continuity to the study. But don't preach.

16. At the end of the Bible discussion, give couples an opportunity to discuss the "For the couples" section and make the application personal. It's important to include this in your group time so that couples don't neglect discussing this material. Of course, sometimes couples may need to discuss the topic long beyond the five minutes of group time allotted, but you can help them get started in the meeting.

17. Encourage group members to work on the "Bonus" section between meetings as a couple or on their own. Give an opportunity during the session for people to talk about what they are learning.

18. End on time.

Many more suggestions and helps on leading a couples group are found in the *Intimate Marriage Leader's Guide*.

COMPONENTS OF SMALL GROUPS

A healthy small group should do more than study the Bible. There are four components to consider as you structure your time together.

Nurture. Small groups help us to grow in our knowledge and love of God. Bible study is the key to making this happen and is the foundation of your small group.

Community. Small groups are a great place to develop deep friendships with other Christians. Allow time for informal interaction before and after each study. Plan activities and games that will help you get to know each other. Spend time having fun together—going on a picnic or cooking dinner together.

Worship and prayer. Your study will be enhanced by spending time praising God together in prayer or song. Pray for each other's needs—and keep track of how God is answering prayer in your group. Ask God to help you to apply what you are learning in your study.

Outreach. Reaching out to others can be a practical way of applying what you are learning, and it will keep your group from becoming self-focused. Host a series of evangelistic discussions for your friends or neighbors. Clean up the yard of an elderly friend. Serve at a soup kitchen together, or spend a day working on a Habitat house.

Many more suggestions and helps in each of these areas are found in *Small Group Idea Book.* Information on building a small group can be found in *The Big Book on Small Groups* (both from InterVarsity Press). Reading through one of these books would be worth your time.

STUDY NOTES

Study 1. Gender Differences. Genesis 3:16-19.

Purpose: To recognize that men and women have different qualities that can complement and enrich each other's lives.

Question 1. Genesis 3:16-19 narrates the curses that God places on Eve, representing women, and Adam, representing men, as a consequence of their rebelling against his will. The difference between the curses against the woman and the man is revealing of gender differences because it appears that they affect women and men in the areas of life most important to them.

The woman's *relationships* are deeply affected. Childbirth will be accompanied by great physical pain, and her relationship with her husband will be marred by a power struggle. The word *desire* in this context most likely connotes "desire to control," not "romantic desire." She desires to control her husband, yet he will master her.

A tragic consequence of sin is the breaking of the original profound unity between women and men pictured in Genesis 2:23-25. Throughout history, in the vast majority of cultures, men have dominated women. And women have been tempted to make relationship their god, to focus their lives on it to the exclusion of developing other dimensions of their humanness.

Question 3. The curse affects Adam in the realm of work. He will struggle with sweat and pain to produce food, will experience failure and futility in his engagement with the world. Even if his work is successful and he can hire people to attend to all the unpalatable tasks, the curse is not lifted. All that he creates will eventually turn to dust. Focusing his sense of security and significance in work will lead to brokenness and frustration.

Question 5. In pursuit of relationship, women may cultivate traits like tenderness, compassion and wisdom. In order to succeed at their work, men will desire strength of mind and body. Women and men will also prize those traits in others. Of course, both women and men can become unbalanced if they cultivate *only* the qualities commonly identified with their gender.

Question 6. The differences do *not* mean that men aren't interested in relationship, or that if a man is relational he is not manly. The same may be said with regard to women and work. There are no ironclad distinctive roles for men and women. Of course, because of their biological makeup women do have a role that men can't share: childbearer. But Scripture nowhere prohibits a woman from entering the workforce (see study four on Prov 31). And certainly men need relationships.

Question 7. It would be boring to marry someone exactly like yourself, and you would never be challenged toward growth if your partner shared all your opinions, tastes, abilities and ways of doing things. A husband and wife whose gifts are complementary can teach and influence each other to cultivate traits that each lacks. If they were *completely* different, however, it would be very difficult to find common ground and mutual understanding.

Question 8. "Variety is the spice of life." Differences can encourage a couple to explore new areas. If the wife is more socially adept, for example, she can help her husband develop relationships with others. Living well in a chaotic world requires a wide array of different abilities, and a couple can complement and strengthen each other.

Study 2. Who's in Charge? Galatians 3:26—4:7.

Purpose: To consider the issue of gender equality or difference with implications for our marriages.

Open. In the current debate the view that we have specific roles set in a hierarchy is called *complementarian.* The view that our equality in Christ extends to the marriage is *egalitarian.*

Question 1. Hierarchies are transformed through relationship with Jesus Christ, demonstrated publicly by baptism. We are made like him. That means that whether one is a free Jewish male or a Gentile woman slave, God is our Father through Jesus Christ—and thus there can be no subordination in Christ.

Question 2. These were all well-established hierarchies in the world of first-century Palestine. Paul is not talking about hierarchies that emerge from Old Testament teaching but those that were rooted in the culture of his day. A free Jewish male was at the top of the social ladder, while a Gentile woman slave would be as low as one could get.

Question 3. Answers may vary according to the community culture in which the discussion is taking place. Possibilities include clergy-laity, rich-poor, upper-lower class, white-minority, and yes, male-female.

Question 4. We have just seen in study one that there are good reasons to affirm gender differences. However, differences do not mandate hierarchy. What makes a man different from a woman does not make a man more valuable than a woman, and vice versa.

Questions 5-6. When one spouse seeks to dominate the other and control them, this can result in their partner's repressing their true feelings or, on the contrary, erupting into conflict. People of either gender can wield power in unhealthy ways, though in most cultures it is men who enjoy more privileges.

Question 7. A marriage between two of God's equal creatures would ideally be marked by mutual submission—a concept to be developed in study three.

Question 8. If we go back to Genesis 1—2, we can see how men and women are treated as equals. They are both created in the image of God. The fact that the woman is the man's "helper" does not imply hierarchy, since God is often elsewhere described as Israel's "helper." The fact that Eve was made from Adam's rib implies mutuality and equality when alternative origins from his head or feet are considered. So the equality between men and women, husbands and wives, is grounded in both creation and redemption.

Study 3. The Ten-Letter Dirty Word. Ephesians 5:21-33; Philippians 2:3-4.

Purpose: To think about how submission fits into the relationships between a husband and wife in the context of Christian marriage.

Question 1. First, note that many modern English translations do a disservice by separating verses 21 and 22, even adding a subject heading between them. In this way many readers miss that the fact that Paul admonishes wives to be submissive in the context of *mutual* submission of all believers to each other. In the light of women's newfound freedom in Christ (see sidebar), it may have been necessary to remind women in particular that they should express their liberation discreetly so as not to alienate nonbelievers around them. In any case, the fact that women are singled out in this passage for special encouragement to submit does not imply that *only* they are to submit. After all, in verses 25-30 husbands are given special encouragement to love their wives, yet we do not believe this relieves wives of their need to love their husbands.

Question 2. A husband is called to love his wife as if she were literally part of his own body, showing her tender care and seeking her well-being.

Question 3. Seek to guide participants away from using their answers to criticize women in their families—for example, "She was constantly complaining. He was a saint to put up with her!"

Question 4. The head does not lord it over others. The model for this is Jesus Christ, whose headship led him to lay down his life for the church. A husband is not head over his wife the way a boss is head over his or her employees. Rather, like Christ, the husband needs to be ready to lay down his life for his wife.

Some New Testament scholars argue that the Greek word translated "head" in this passage means "source" rather than implying authority. This fits well with Paul's reminder to the husband to care for his wife as he cares for his own body. Remember, in the Genesis 2 creation story Eve is formed from Adam's body, and thus he is her source.

Question 5. Relational totalitarianism produces great resentment. After all, a husband who dominates a wife or a wife who dominates her husband squashes an equal being who is created in the image of God. Any compliance is then only a mechanical obedience, not a spontaneous submission motivated by love. The marriage relationship was not designed to leave one partner with little or no say.

Question 6. If a husband never shows any interest in leading his wife or the wife in leading her husband, then the spouse will feel frustrated and unloved. This presumes, of course, that the leading is toward God.

Question 7. To submit to another person means to yield one's individual will to her or his good. Submission does not mean always doing what the other person says; in fact, sometimes it means requiring something from the other person. The key point is that one who submits is giving up self-interest in the interest of the betterment, the growing into godliness, of the other.

Question 8. The kind of relationship described in these verses is selfless and other-centered. When both husband and wife have this attitude toward one another, the result is that both grow in glory and in their relationship with God. As that relationship strengthens, so does their bond.

For the Couple. Sarah is held up as a model of submission. This is interesting and illuminating because a review of her life (Gen 11:27—23:20) indicates that she was anything but a doormat. The apostle Peter considers this woman, who sometimes was in Abraham's face, to be a paragon of submission.

Bonus. Jesus' life is characterized by submission to the church. He does not seek his way, but he lives and dies for the good of the church.

Study 4. The Godly Wife. Proverbs 31:10-31.

Purpose: To explore the qualities of a godly wife.

Question 1. It is likely that women especially will be overwhelmed by the sheer enormity of the woman's tasks. She is indeed "energetic and strong, a hard worker" (31:17). However, later in the study, we will bring out the fact that this text isn't a catalog of tasks to be completed by every woman.

Question 2. Some may be surprised by the fact that the woman not only cares for her family but also works hard at commerce and agriculture. Some may be surprised that the woman who is described is obviously from the upper class and may question whether women who are not so well off can do what she does. Others may be surprised that sex is not mentioned in the text. The leader may want to follow up in any of these areas.

Question 3. Ask that only the women in the group respond to this question. Probably some women will find it oppressive, as they wrongly read the list of the woman's activities as things they must do. Not all women are as energetic and strong as this woman. On the other hand, other women, particularly those who have been told that women have very circumscribed roles in the world, will find this picture liberating.

Question 4. Certainly no woman is required to do all the things this woman is described as doing. Nonetheless, modern couples can learn a lot from this passage. For one thing, it presents a picture of a wife whose energies are united with her husband's to push back the chaos of life. She works with him, not against him. Of course the husband is pictured as a wise man himself, someone who sits in the gate—a position of great importance, power and responsibility in the ancient Near East. It implies that he is a hard worker as well. This passage also disrupts the typical evangelical Christian stereotype of an ideal woman as someone who just stays at home, minds the children and satisfies her husband. The Proverbs woman's first responsibility *is* her family, and both her husband and her children praise her. But in the service of her family she is in the public square wheeling and dealing. She is concerned not only with her family's material needs but with their psychological and spiritual needs as well. In addition, she is concerned with societal problems: she cares for the poor (v. 20). This indeed is some woman, a model to be emulated.

Question 5. The poem leaves us in no doubt, nor does the rest of the book of Proverbs. All throughout Proverbs, beginning in 1:7, we are reminded that "fear of the LORD is the beginning of knowledge." This woman epitomizes this truth.

Question 6. Charm and beauty are not that important to a marriage relationship. In fact elsewhere in Proverbs the father warns his son about the deceptive nature of flattery and beauty. These are superficial qualities that may mask a horrible personality. As Proverbs 11:22 says, "A woman who is beautiful but lacks discretion is like a gold ring in a pig's snout." Men sometimes can't see the pig behind the attractive gold ring. A relationship built on the foundation of beauty and charm can't last, because these qualities diminish over time.

All this said, beauty is not to be completely despised. The Song of Songs keeps us from making that rash conclusion. However, there is no question that its importance is only secondary.

Question 8. After reading this description, many people may conclude that no one can find such a woman because such superhuman people don't exist! We do have to conclude that this picture is something of an ideal that imperfect human beings cannot fully live up to. Perhaps, though, the expected answer is anticipated in Proverbs 19:14: a good wife is a gift from God.

Bonus. The woman has made a sentimental statement about women's role in bearing children. The suggestion is that women have value *if* they give birth to boys who grow up to be admired!

Jesus does not devalue childbearing, but he calls women to be first and foremost his disciples (look back at Prov 31:30). In his day only men were considered to be "disciple material" as students of rabbis, and women who were unable to bear sons were pitied. So in his apparently simple statement Jesus is honoring women and greatly expanding their horizons.

Fortunately, in Western cultures today most women are not under pressure to bear sons to prove their worth. Unfortunately, Western cultures now tend toward a strange mix of both devaluing parenting and making an idol of it. (Idols are useful for marketing products.) The church generally seeks to elevate motherhood, but this can leave single or infertile women feeling less than complete.

Perhaps a church's women's ministry could be led by a team that includes single and married women, some who pursue a career and some who stay home with small children. The goal should be to avoid focusing on any one part of women's roles or identity and instead to encourage women to "hear the word of God and obey it!"

Study 5. The Godly Husband. Psalm 112.

Purpose: To explore the qualities of a godly husband.

Question 1. The psalm begins with a description of the godly man as one who fears the Lord. As for the godly woman, this seems to be the foundational character of the godly man and presumably the trait that should be foremost in a woman's mind as she thinks of what she desires in a husband.

Question 2. Both place ultimate importance on fear of the

Lord. If both a husband and a wife have their priorities straight, then it deepens a relationship. Further, both the godly man and the godly woman are ethical and are generous toward others who need help (v. 9). Because of their confidence in God, they do not fear the future (v. 7). The children of the godly couple are blessed by their parents (v. 2).

Question 3. Have only the men in group respond to this question.

Question 4. Among other things, a godly husband who fears only the Lord can give confidence to his wife. If a husband is afraid of work, relationships, life in general, it can't help but unsettle his wife (and vice versa). Also, a man who fears the Lord obeys God's commands, so his wife can be assured that her husband will be faithful.

Question 5. There is nothing here about a man's good looks or virility. It is not that these are totally irrelevant. After all, the Song of Songs reflects on the physical attractiveness of both the man and the woman. However, it does serve to tell us something about priorities. By silence, Psalm 112 seems to be teaching the same thing as Proverbs 31:30: "Charm is deceptive, and beauty does not last; but a woman who fears the LORD will be greatly praised."

Question 6. Godly men reflect many of the traits of their Maker. The Lord is righteous, and so are they (compare Ps 111:3 with 112:4). He and they are gracious and merciful (the same Hebrew words are found in Ps 111:4 and 112:4, though translated "generous" and "compassionate" in the second psalm). He is just and good, and so are they (111:7 and 112:5).

Question 7. The better we know God, the better we can reflect godly traits. We come to know God intimately through reading his Word and through prayer. In particular we should study the Gospels, where we learn about how God Incarnate thought and acted.

Study 6. Reflecting the Glory of God Together. Joshua 5:13-15; Psalm 131.

Purpose: To realize that both males and females are created in the image of God and thus both reflect God's glory.

Question 1. It is God himself, the captain of the heavenly armies. This is made clear by the fact that Joshua must take his sandals off in his presence (which reminds us of Moses at the burning bush in Ex 3). Furthermore, Joshua bows deeply to this figure in a way that would be appropriate only if the man represented God.

Question 2. For those whose mental image of God tends toward "feminine" and nurturing (like the image of Ps 131), this picture may be jarring. For others it will seem quite appropriate. One goal of this study is for people to be reminded that our views of God are usually too limited.

Question 3. We learn that God is a warrior who fights for his people against their enemies. He is not on our side, nor is he against us; he fights solely for the glory of God. When we fight for God's glory and not our own, we are not so much a friend as a fellow warrior for God.

Question 4. God is not male. But this story does tell us that God may be adequately and partially represented by a male warrior. The picture also tells us that men are warriors. They fight against the chaos around them. In Old Testament times warfare often took a physical form, but in the New Testament, the time we live in today, our warfare is exclusively spiritual (Eph 6:10-20). Men are called to be spiritual warriors today.

Question 5. The image is subtle and complex but in no doubt. The psalmist is expressing his contented trust in God. He says that he rests in God the way a weaned child rests with its mother.

Question 6. An unweaned child easily gets restless in its mother's arms. The mother, after all, is the child's source of food, so a nursing baby can get awfully fidgety when Mom is holding it. A weaned child can rest more comfortably.

Question 7. God is not female. But the psalm does tell us that God may be adequately and partially represented by a mother. The picture also tells us that women are relational and nurturing. They protect and nourish. They provide comfort and compassion.

Question 8. It reminds us that marriage is a union of two equals. It reminds us that each bears the image of God and each reflects God to the other. It should instill in the couple an intense love and respect for each other.

Bonus. As the New Testament reveals (Eph 5:23), the husband is the "head" of the wife, and that is appropriate for God in relationship with his people. We have also already seen that "headship" denotes the first to sacrifice for the other, the first to submit to the well-being of the other. Still, this image does not mean that somehow males are closer to the essence of who God is. The fact that marriage is used in Revelation 19 and in many other passages to picture our relationship with God shows just how important, intensely intimate and exclusive that relationship is.